Knowledge, Forms, the Aviary

Winner of the
Sawtooth Poetry Prize
2005

Carolyn Forché, judge

Knowledge, Forms, the Aviary

Karla Kelsey

AHSAHTA PRESS

Boise State University • Boise • Idaho • 2006

Ahsahta Press, Boise State University
Boise, Idaho 83725
http://ahsahtapress.boisestate.edu

Copyright © 2006 by Karla Kelsey
Printed in the United States of America
Cover art and design by Quemadura
Author photograph by Peter Strange Yumi
Book design by Janet Holmes
First printing January 2006
ISBN 0-916272-87-7

Library of Congress Cataloging-in-Publication Data

Kelsey, Karla.
   Knowledge, forms, the aviary / Karla Kelsey.
      p. cm.
   "Winner of the Sawtooth Poetry Prize, 2005."
   ISBN 0-916272-87-7 (pbk. : alk. paper)
   I. Title.
PS3611.E473K58 2006
811'.6--DC22

                              2005025537

ACKNOWLEDGMENTS

Grateful acknowledgment is made to the editors of *Verse, Fence, 26, Boston Review, Chimera Review, GutCult,* and *Double Room,* where some of the poems in this book originally appeared. To my family, friends, and teachers—for your kindness, patience, and encouragement—thank you.

For Peter and our walks

Contents

Knowledge, Forms, The Aviary is a lyric enactment of the confluence of thought, language and possibility, embarking from Plato's *Theaetetus,* where *in the mind of each…there is an aviary,* a flock of knowledges beating wings against (only) apparent confines, as the mind beholds and captures knowledges in turn, various in form, able to be fleetingly caged but not possessed. This is a poetry that resists possession of world by mind with all that this implies for the dominions of power; it is a poetry that refuses the cumulative acquisition of experience, but rather thinks toward and through our knowing *the beyond and between*—not only what is, but what is (apparently) not. This resistance is at once philosophical and political, though not systematic, yet the implications for human relation to world are clear. Kelsey writes what it is to know, of *what we become/ when the universe is seen in lights of its generation.* We are, in this work, in the midst of things, and as Plato's Socrates has it, *the eye becomes filled with vision and now sees, and becomes, not vision but a seeing eye.* Kelsey's gift is for the inter-subjective lyric, the "we" of interdependence. *For,* she writes, *if earth is the center of the body, heaven is the center of the soul….We are her species. We are her parts.* The genius of this work is in its formal embodiment of epistemology: the layerings and repetitions, asterisks and spacings, and the ways in which the language of the senses remains in such flux that no recurring image returns as it was, but rather is changed by the shimmer of perceptual encounter. As phenomenologist Merleau-Ponty has understood, "If we set ourselves to see as things the intervals between them, the appearance of the world would be just as strikingly altered…there would not be simply the same elements differently related, the same sensations differently associated…but in truth another world." This is what Kelsey has given us in lyric form: another world, wherein the reader may enter and become awake.

Carolyn Forché
Judge, 2005 Sawtooth Poetry Prize

Soc. Well, may not a man "possess" and yet not "have" knowledge in the sense of which I am speaking? As you may suppose a man to have caught wild birds—doves or any other birds—and to be keeping them in an aviary which he has constructed at home; and then we might say, in one sense, that he always has them because he possesses them, might we not?

Theaet. Yes.

Soc. And yet, in another sense, he has none of them; but he has power over them, and has them under his hand in an enclosure of his own, and can take and have them whenever he likes; he can catch any which he likes, and again let them go, and he may do this as often as he pleases.

Theaet. True.

Soc. Once more, then, as in what preceded, we make a sort of waxen figment in the mind, so let us now suppose that in the mind of each man there is an aviary of all sorts of birds—some flocking together apart from the rest, others in small groups, others solitary, flying anywhere and everywhere.

Theaet. Let us imagine that done; what is to follow?

Soc. We may suppose this receptacle to be empty while we are young, and that the birds are kinds of knowledge; when a man has gotten and detained in the enclosure any of those different kinds of knowledge, then he may be said to have learned or discovered the thing of which that knowledge is: and this is to know.

Theaet. Granted.

Soc. And again, when any one wishes to catch any of these knowledges or sciences, and hold any of them after he has taken them, and again to let them go, consider how he will express that; will he describe the "catching" of them and the original "possession" in the same words?

--Plato, *Theaetetus*

*f*LOOD/*f*OLD

*

*

*

*

*

*

into the street making
this the movement. What
we call home comprised
into lake-ripple
and pictured. Sold
unto a title of time, of
composition
into the back of the chair
a waiting within
the network: a visor
and a mask

*

*

*

are whispering rooms,
the will to name
fallen in between Sunday
and Monday. Without
the street, meter gone, I call

the moment blue-green
prescribed into the arc
of sun to sky

                                        *

                                        *

                                        *

in the small
valley, created
in sounds and
a slowing, the possibility
of flight marked
by wind
in the flag. Marked
by the spaces
between buildings,

                                        *

                                        *

                                        *

a line streaming, the crack
in the sky holding. This
is no ordinary eye site. Described,
the yellow bench
under the crabapple. Two

women waiting
and one turns
and the other. Still
as in found
deep in sand. As in
the layer of willing

*

*

*

daily begun from.
The blue paper crane
hangs in the tree,
arc of thrust and drag. You
left plumed. You
arrived telling of golden sands
and a golden sea, sidereal navigation
bringing the bird home
over bright blooms
of fire, explosion

*

*

*

in the night, this imprint
now faded, the mark

of two faces, hands
brought to the thorn. Step
here and the game
wounds to shadow
and porch light, home
a movement of wind
though the path
of migration
alters

*

*

*

*

*

*

*

*

*

*

*

*

*

*

*

*

*

a wave of waiting
for the break

in breath up-scaled
to the top of the tower's
singed window

*

*

*

*

—called to the hillside—

the engravings augment—

small stone—crosses—

*

they tell us to be—not abandoned

—but cross-hatched in hope—

as in a pattern—washed over us—

—washing over our—

*

orange—with

—shades of—

as at the free project—setting out chairs

between—trees configured

—into meeting places—

*

*

I heard him through—

phrases of clouds—

and though—fretted here

*

—with brain-patterns—

and pocked with—

what I know not—

*

my inner rhythm—

and clanging—

over-riding—

from trains—and   *

—in theory—the orange

—brightening this—

*   calling to seep—

through our irises—

holding us—

*

—and holding—pigmented—
            with what has been—

                    *

    —this vista—of crosses—though there are
                —strong arms and the wall

                    *

                cool—to your cheek—phrases of
                        consolation—limp and—

                    *

            wash them over—with a
    paler shade of blue—

                    *

            and the pattern—
of your own—breath—

                    *

*

gone—and in the project—

*

we sit in these chairs—bolted to the ground—

*

patch of dirt and yellow—

*

snow lilies—

*

of inner rhythm—shown

*

on the screens—

*

we add orange to them—

*

then stripes—

*

then the paler—

*

shades of blue—constructed

*

this way—of edges

*

—of small crosses and clouds—

*

we are—pinned to the hill—the night

*

—bridgeless against sky

*

*

*

*

*

*

*

*

*

*

And breaking into crested elements—the orchid

exposed, fringed so far from

the road—distant explosion writing the eye in

the middle of what we have found

*

*

*

*

*

*

*

    —brilliant orange parts all
    incurved and concaved—they conceal

    us under the dome of the
    upper sepal—yet

*

*

*

*

*

displayed conspicuously below. Instead of

being patient—as most of them—

growing into firmer red and waiting

for defense missionaries to arrive—we saw

the first blossom—the first light of the stroking firmer sod—we fell

apart in the wake of reed grass—

*

*

*

*

*

at the entrance we heard
the sound of curlews—

the end of the red road
polished with wet and sun

*

*

*

*

*

nearly circular—
and strongly concaved—
the lateral pair spared

*

*

*

*

*

taken home to the yellow fringed
flares darting over the domes
of our city—close to the sea and stepping
we must abandon

*

*

*

*

*

the upper one bent
forward over the column, hold—
we hold none of them
so strongly—for the answers—
have gone

*

*

*

*

*

        —and in the car, to escape them
though there were not many
and I—merely one—my
restraint rotted

*

*

*

*

*

*

        rich orange
        inflorescence portends
        making way back from
        the Atlantic—symbol
        of the flower after
        blooming

*

*

*

*

*

after the scene alters the wind
shield shatters—

*

*

*

*

*

branches there disappearing
into tell me—all about—
the individual mites—the burnt tree
you will pass beneath

*

*

*

*

*

*

*

*

(coda of the olive tree, pure, pointed under radio frequency we can hear meteors and the abandoned city wasting in the valley of white sands, fed under the flares gone tracing another life, held here tied, the kite string to metal elements rusting

*

*

*

*

*

*

*

*

*

*

gone into the flickering
of the image-bird, into this is the public garden and we walked
picking up seed and twisting it
into safe foil packages. Into accident

*

*

*

*

*

*

I have willed the account to the most obscure
member. Milk white distance; delivering the one

from the one in the moment the peacock
crosses our path

*

*

*

she has found something at last to say. Delivered

*

*

*

*

from the parched element. Toy
medium of plastic soldiers
in the second degree. Described

*

*

*

*

as the ocean wailing and I felt
                          like crystal
                          and iron
                          in the air:
                          crisp and
                          I thought
                          I caught I
                          darting here
                          discernable
                          in this era of
                          revolution

                                    *

                                    *

                                    *

                                    *

                                    *

              a sentence for the broken jaw
and pier lights beckoning
              off water, we have been called
                          and our thoughts drift, lapping

                                    *

                                    *

*

*

*

       thought from memory and reading. I must ask you why
this should be spoken of in terms
    of possession: the *I go* or *I went* of the face
      the call of a bird, of grace

*

*

*

*

*

while at the edges, singing, not far
    from the public garden, not far
from the walk through the zoo
    scattering peanut shells as the light
dims. Shadow-printed and

*

*

*

*

*

marked: we were here and
there was a
trembling
to the
sky
as trucks rolled
through
and through
what was re-
named *our valley*

*

*

*

*

And inside the room her needs awaiting unto what has and hasn't
been done before over the edge of the circumspect as we counter the bird
in the glass while in the image she arrays herself in light or
in a series of checkings and a flourishing use of the atomizer

all to have left just a moment as a pane of glass
balancing on its edge.

                              *

                              *

                              *

                              *

                              *

These things I have rubbed with a soft cloth
for the gleam in them remembering the street outside
and the way she said "hero" as she once said "green in my hand"
upon seeing the park these simple utterances I envy
walking in language even when the song refuses to through.

                              *

                              *

                              *

                              *

                              *

Little and in light or in luck the glass gleams sharded
or not though more intense when sun strikes windshields

in the parking lot as I am looking for her and the image
of a complete finding in this reflection curved into the shadow of the lean.

*

*

*

*

*

Melted back into the simple, word
of order, the sweeping sound of
sweeping up piles of dust and glass.

*

*

*

*

to relinquish the shadow
bird, these sands and the breakers. Sound
of it. Sound of her there
which means the wind whipping
her skirt. On the edge of these things what is thought
is held and twisted around in the mind as the mint

or stone sucked softly in the mouth a disintegration
of array but nevertheless a disintegration.

                              *

                              *

                              *

                              *

The movement of perfection between scent and sight
attained and then lost, thought not as an escalation of vision or the smell
of darkness she calls acrid and leading to the stilled waters, as sometimes
these elements are clear and I can tell you this is the way she said it would be
and this is the way that it is, flocking and the sound of fans whirring low,
and at other times the image stills, and the thought falls blurred,
we know this if we can say we know anything, rehearsed by often and by many.

                              *

                              *

                              *

                              *

Halting into the mouth I thought
the image of the bird would sing but it wouldn't
though the mouth says I am content now with domestic things

the sound of the broom on the floor body moving
the way a woman's body has been seen moving
a simpler song and more sweet some would say when heard or read
as the birds wake and there is no reason for waking oneself
on a day like this beginning in curtain light and oranges.

*

*

*

*

*

*

*

*

*

The shine having lost
and marked the stone is less a part
of the stone than its blackness though
the shine is part of the day part of the bird squawking
and flying over x's, power lines.

*

*

*

Excised into glory   flower   the pattern
       in the motion of the hand
       is the motion of the arm
           a leaf and livid shadow, some sort of there

*

constructed in piles of hardened earth

*

       and, so, here remembered, sleep,
       though tomorrow may not be so folded,
           an absence of flooding in these lands

*

              crystalline in our ocean-fallow,
               the sea bed set into ridges
             of rock, a natural variegation.
          In this version we are walking here
          and so listed into new numbers
      or other versions of having caught the quaking

                                    *

elementals of some design
            of what will be held
            red in the eye   feather
            of molting
                        patches in the hand

                                    *

                        blended, or to soothe another
                                    form of vision along the lines of eye
                                    sight arcing toward

                                    *

the refinery, at night, all aglow

                        in orange light smoke pummeling upwards

                                    *

                                    *

                                    *

                                    *

                                    *

                                    *

Gone to the window, light there wood-glossy and in non-repose

                                        *

As in pick up the seeds and throw them into the street

                                        *

As in 1 color, gone gold and so seeing, all blurred around edges and walking

                                        *

Another sort of line this time, message burnt into the gold

                                        *

Into the edges and a man in the street breaking bottle after bottle

                                        *

                                        *

                                        *

                                        *

And so this to explain the glittering splash of sidewalk, such a color or lapping

                                        *

At the river mouth, or an aquarium in the window stored, this new aperture

*

Not just a hole to see through but blasted man-sized to step through

*

Into the other room, call it treason, call it a certain element

*

Of shimmering given off by impressions and the glowing

*

*

*

*

As if there were not the possibility of any other name for the color

*

Formulated in the mind, an original shock of orange

*

None other like it from sunset to tangerine, rendered by your feeling forth

*

Of color sensations, taut wires between them outlining new objects of space

*

Coined visible, invisible, or an alternate scraping of rust

*

*

*

*

*

*

*

*

*

along the edges
of the window, river, winnow quiver
embedded   in
          the book   of knowledge

yet gone along the siding. These layers folded
into a "yes," rivers of ore in the land,

record of the atom split, mountain from ridge breaking
towards the deep and other modes
of transformation: *the perspective is*
                                        in the body

                                        *

                                        *

                                        *

                                        *

                                        *

Flurry off and double sited we were
walking, that moment, down the street
          and we were walking that moment

                                        *

                                        *

escaped into air, wings the color of
no color, as in divined without a name without

*

*

*

*

*

*

*

*

*

Gone to the window, light there wood-glossy/ Miller introduces Melus: The Apple Tree

*

As in pick up the seeds and throw them into/ The Characters of this particular

*

As in 1 color, gone gold and so seeing / the 1731 edition of *The Gardener's Dictionary* tells

Another sort of line this time, message burnt/ are such that The Tree grows very large

*

Into the edges and a man in the street breaking/ the Branches spread,

*

/(and are more depressed than

*

/those of the Pear Tree);

*

/the Flowers consist

*

And so this to explain the glittering splash / of five Leaves, which expand

*

At the river mouth, or an aquarium in the window / in the form of a Rose,

*

Not just a hole to see through /thus approximating Characters of other varietals,

*

Into the other room, call it treason, call it / the Fruit is hollowed about the Footstalk

*

Of shimmering given off by impressions and / is for the most Part roundish,

*

/ and is umbillicated

*

/at the Top,

*

/is Fleshy,

*

As if there were not the possibility / divided into five Cells or Partitions, as

*

Formulated in the mind, an original shock of / a building is divided into apartments, as

*

None other like it from sunset/ apartments are divided into rooms, as the page

*

Of color sensations/ is divided into sections and the name of each tree into each section,

*

Coined visible, invisible/ named, as in each fruit of the Melus, is lodg'd, one oblong seed

*

*

*

*

*

a waking back into
the slanting meadow and sun caught
in the corner

*

*

*

*

*

the names attached with twisting delicate

wire tied to the stone, the names
of the stone indicating what is elemental to it,
elemental to us...*mineral, granite, pyrite*

*

*

Detached from its moment,
the rose, leafy flower cup,
becomes an oblong fleshy fruit

petals falling and telling
into the earth, the slant

warm field,
no cloud
steals,
for the rose
hath pinnated
leaves. Set

inside its moment, glass vase and
reflecting upon a glossy surface,
the rose

of my rose
is like other
matters
of the spirit,
its name tells

*

*

*

*

*

Gone to the window, light there murky and the view closed

*

Asking to pick up the seeds and explode them into the street

*

As in 1 color, gone gold and so searing, sharp at the edges and waltzing

*

Another sort of line this time, message burnt into the cold

*

Into edges and flight thrust up trying to make them meet, shaking leaf after leaf

*

rust between molting, cries, feathers marked for the cage,

*

raging nocturnal migration via stellar navigation

*

entirely white, no aigrettes on the back this time

*

And so this to explain the glittering slash of sidewalk, such a lover or a lacking

*

At the river mouth, or an aquarium in the window stored in this new aperture

*

Not just a hole to see through but out-blasted, capsized to seep through

*

Into the outer room, call it treason, call it a feathered lament

*

Of particles shriven by impressions and the fluttering

*

during the step between one side of the walk and the other

*

they lit from their trees, caught in cold-tongued lightning,

*

wind and air soldered, flight stalled, ordered to an opening and then gone

*

As if there were not the possibility of any other name for the bird

*

Form striated in the bind, an original shock of orange

*

None other like it from sunset to tangerine, rendered by a freeing forth

*

Of feather sensations, taut wires between them out-limning new objects of space

*

Coined visible, invisible, or an alternate scraping of trust

*

and through a crack in the sky, the mind

*

draws a relation between patterns

*

of bones and the colors feathering them

*

*

*

of yellowing consolation: *order is added*
to the weak shrub
when the bloom is taken away.

*

*

*

*

*

The seeing unto, as in some carry. Others, the way of it

(in terms of a name it has been called) becomes

the walking measure, elliptical escaping. Window of sky

44

known in cloud and cloud drifting. Or attachment to

seething, in memory, of elements, the seeds of this plain

and through the air. Or to it

posturing lament or what we become

when the universe is seen in light of its generation, elevation

*

of knowing how, as when mica, sprig, and the other side

of the painted wall are revealed on bright canvas

or some other sort of proffering

*

coins taken
        from the tops of eyes or
the stark blight
        of frost. Brown, rust
        lingering there in the reeds,

oh rustle into what is given and
prepared for the meeting:
let it all in

*

Gone now the linden, light wears heart-tossing and in none reposed

*

The quick in our seeds and thrown down by our feet

*

As in one-another, love cold and so seeping, all burned-out hedges and talking

*

Another sordid line this time, message breaking into the cold

*

In two, edges and a man trying to make them meet, breaking model after model

*

No other like this from Sun City to Tangiers, rendered by your freeing forth

*

Of older ululations, taut fires between us outlining new objects of place

*

Coined visceral, indivisible, or an alternate raping of dust

*

And so this to explain the glittering slash of sidewalk, such another, or a lapping

*

At the quiver's mouth, or an aviary for a window, this new aperture

*

Not just a lull to be through but lasting land-prized to meet you

*

Into the loom, call it a season, call it a personal bent

*

Of shivering tossed off by depression and an alternate flowering

*

Long after the wind, how, light there flood-glossing as in the decomposed

*

As in pick up the need, encode it into the street

*

As in one older, lone gold and so searing, all blurred-around edges and waltzing

*

As if, there, wearing the ability of any lover's fame for the other

*

Form mutilated in the mind as in an original crop of spores

*

And others like it, form un-set to twist marine up-ended by your fraying

*

Of nether relations, taut wires between them out limning new objections of space

*

Coined lisible, un-kissable, or an alternate prating of lust

*

And so missed to explain the slivering clash on the sidewalk, such dolor or collapsing

*

Of the river mouth or an unwary wind storming this blue aperture

*

Not just a hole to see through but out-blasted, capsized to steep through

*

Into the outer rooms, we call it reason, we call it a tin lament

*

*

*

*

*

*

*

*

*

*

*

*

CONTAINMENT AND *f*RACTURE

*

*

*

THE REPORT IS HERE as the dunes are, made useful unto a harmonics of image blocking, mountains hedging up as if a folded line of municipalities fleeing. It was on the road from here that it happened, one and one and nothing left on the shelves to pilfer

and light leaking from under doorways to know we are home by, to ask a borrowing as branches fall and power lines go down around the river. I write the fields in our hands and what was warranted,

sacrificed as in the held blood of the temple. This has come out of red set against black so that the end of the red is the end of the black. The key's in, invasion granted over borders and fields of live wires, these lines buried deep in sands

OF AFTER THE MARK of hip on hip on hand. A standard of any body. A market of going towards the green to sing again the news of day done over breakers or shallows. The marking here of *what I meant* or *we were so held by decision,* as in the kindling of heat distilled and pointing us toward the day-faded moon. I say *this is a listing* and you, these weedings and selfish the world if it does not better us, make us as suns upon open metallic parts. The yard, yawning, and what we have been led by has gone out of context and out of the eye-inspired movement of *I choose* or *I am a this but not that*, plush and smooth as in the center of a fruit

AND THE LUNG, intended to be dramatic in its motion, bird-thought confined to inner writing as the virus circulates among natural hosts. The element gone to our breathing, isolated from terns, we walk through daily sickness, ten dead on the path through the park. The virus circulates, carried through wiring. Key to containing the outbreak is a culling of those exposed, a vision of preparation in the pile of burned bones, feather ash, fire of skin made to happen amidst the room, the blown-glass bird tied to a ribbon, slight movement when there is breeze. These moments are working our forgiveness, patients treated and isolated as the flutter in the lung, the burning brush

I WAS WORKING THE FREE RADICALS, the delay, looking for a method in this desire of constituting a whole. As if to reconstruct an imagined world in shades of red seen through light particles of varying density. Red, darker red, orange-red, air—as in being given an audience and so the ability to perform the whole, the parts thereof, the keening. Allowing a "her" into the abstraction arrests it for a moment. This abstraction has been arrested as a form of grace, light in ash-dense air gilds trees. We are not satisfied.

Patches of sky. Which brings us the new entity formed and named by metaphor for the sake of the object suspended, the noblest part of earth, before we find it blowing so away, as if a statue, not of earth, but of trees charred to cinder. Red. Or we can take the line of our fallen state. Darker red. For if earth is the center of the body, heaven is the center of the soul, with its planned moving, mutability conceded for the pattern, for a constant assurance of species and her parts. Orange-red. We are her species. We are her parts. The abstraction loses its arrest and we wake to the story of the flying bird, now held in her hand and slit down the middle

OVERLOAD OF PALM IN THE LINES, we say veering and excise. Of the river, gardens on either side. Or it was a garden and the ford overflown, splitting, causing sides. Weeds out, the wrought iron rested. These were gates and so rusted and passing by on the lawn. Elemental of what is dispersed into air, radial display, our liquid sky, as in painted. Tie the flies and we are one and one through fire. Isn't that nice. And mires counted, re-counted. Down and out, coping with the monitor, the green eye I call you back through to the spilt garden, seed-pods, liquid, sky

our going into, called inter-atmospheric arms gesturing out and out as in a flicking action as in the ugly word haloing your head. Multiplying by twos, images not exactly mirrored. Displayed. We counted down. Liquid to sky to garden and garden-split-rotting. Can we coin it mirror-like, though they have run unto the ocean. Or we have run to the ocean, moment, laundry-lines swaying like the river like the heat up-rising the tarmac. Visible. While we pin and un-pin to the widow sash. Eyes rested

the delay of your thorough going arm. Radial. Inquisitive names, a gesture, a look of the eyes. Inquisitive names gesture: look at her eyes. The split sided, the seeding, the sound now of river of line on the map the river drawing through the gesture through the arms to stay here. For a bitter-longer. Radial. As in the mirror-prayer we say the banks, the river, pattern of sun blinking on and on and off to stay our looking for. Cemented into image and going down to tributary, to ocean, down to. The sand bar. Sunken ships called a graveyard gesturing towards the intentional though folded into an inquiry about the hold

OF UNDER THE ASH AND SO, as they say, weeping. Along a river. Along another vein, arm, hand, listing the light inconsequential, factored by duty and done up in the new winds. In the temperature washing the orange out of it with shades of blue. Then paler blue then something approaching white or nothing, the page, the bone gone back to the originary plan of an aviary built with mesh siding, illusioning the possibility of flight. Soft walls, soft keeping us here

POCKET OF VALLEY full of clouds though cement spikes mica around us and you perform a noticing, held and counted to a hundred and so holding the air, the wrought iron railing, to tell me this is not simply a record of inner stearin, of the flexible fabric pinned up as in a wing as in the warmth of the valley cooled to. Not an any-other held, levering it up, but the glint of sun on the bridge, metallic shine, texture felt as it circulates and is called. Molded to fit inside a specific point and my eyes crater here at the bottom of this moment of to feel and go slack around edges, not to mention the smell of skin of thin clouds skirting these mountains

hands folded. Giving a feeling of solidarity to. Trestled and retold to the girders, we are here at the edge of land folding into land. As the sun folds. Watch the flock lift and say *I uncover you*, the cover gone back through and breaking solidarity into elements told in the forms our old eyes broke. And so vesseled and so carried over the valley not knowing the direction, steep incline, fear in the map where our river had been. Numbers mark the spot and we are held to a remembrance of what is tamped down beyond soil and the shallows. As the molting begins, we are cited to a mapped place, starred in the dirt as an offering.

ACROSS THE STREET LIGHT-FORMS hang in trees, branches bare and scaled, and as remaining leaves caught in frost curl, lung forms hang inside us and the heater buzzes and a bird calls so long and so forth. We are known by these things like a painted aviary or the inside of this shedding

light, the easy disaster come forth to weep and so to seed the fallow land. Sun and wind whisk the curtains with cold and what becomes important is that these are our hands, our handled areas of light, patterning this

or the paths they make in the sky or on the canvas given up to a likening rendered in paint and stillness, the easy disaster pictured as a stranger, here, standing so lean and cool to the touch as we concentrate on the bus stop framed by the window and the streetlights click off into another variation of dawning

THIS IS WHAT I SEE through false eyes and a hole in the siding. A gape and then flooding. A gape in the ribs and then flooding called breath. Then the red curtain and phrase of one and one. As if painted, the sky approaching sunset, duration of fire. Smoke fills our lungs as we mount, two by two along the wooden railing. Placed, we receive bouquets of patience. The strum of. And guitar,

garden dry wall crumbled and branches a-fade, fading. The call outlined with an arc of birds in the sky. Circling. Felt in my hair, a moment, then hands put to. Well of the eyes. We stoop and they sweep the tin siding, the roofing patented green. For the lost. This is the way that it has to be. As in her eyes on the edges of her lower lids. For the sight lines and valley over brilliant blue battering. A falling. Flag foment and the pages crease. And, creasing, share over the marble and granite sun. Over forms accidentally there.

The moment clouds enter the building, in the outline of our shadows. Don't ask how this occurs, akin to roses, browning along edges. Trees, the necessary distance from flames. We write them off shore, securing the mind's eye. As in his aviary birds of knowledge fly captive, saved from asphyxiation. A way of leaving the field of snow and fire while flying forward without a chance for adjustment, nothing caught in the clearing

WORDS TO SAY and or listing or there is no mal intent. Another sort of mahogany, he keeps it vertical as in encased in a glass tube felling the layers up and then down, working with his hands on the sides of it. To say it is invisible. To say it follows a pattern of duty and redbud trees in the distance. There is no mal intent only the zero of. And the layers up and then down become confusing as the man in the moon, a sorrow like the satellite dish and some words the texture of violets. And so to say, to veer off in a delicate corner where the light is kind and I can re-play and re-say as he moves up and down and for a moment pauses, arm muscles quivering in glossy air

*i*MPRESSION, *f*LUX, CONTIGUITY

*

*

*

LISTING NOW FOR TOKENS, for order—
the sepal-flower grown
in back lots. Shrub and baseball bat.
Pinned. The pennant gone wavering now, gone into truck-

sounds and magnetic fields absorbing. It went and it goes.
We went and we go, not the would have, there,
umbrella hinged up like a wing

over-scouting and wavelets scudding.
Beyond the lot, vision caught my holy in the new saint. New
picture new page of the martyred. Mated. Dragonflies hover
and we topple

to the sound of purity given up
to our making. We can call if we must, the leaves in, canopy
shaking. This is sight this is sound. Paying it—

replaying it then. Where there are grooves in the record
our voices die into hovering
telling us maybe we are off-wind. This I write. Tightened

into *I am not so,* not a seeming although there is
a sound and image accordance and though this
is an eye-piece. Pierced for the gathering, maybe, or hum.
Anything to remember ourselves by

though when we say it, what do we mean, tone, curve of upper lip, by
this I would coin it
cruel and glassy. So under the hollows we go
to find the holy wood, to back-track to moisture
and the lichen and the Styrofoam cup

capitalized into weather-breath. Berthed. Your notion of my
satellite, wind beating the rubberized fabric to a new sound
of textile and telling you this is a relation

among relations, air feeling October and the walk
along the ridge. To get to. Casting over two
by two from the window and wanting it all to be figured up
into sense for the X, for the apparatus. For the eyes

to tell to the ears beyond the black
and white image of a hatted man on his horse

IN THE AVIARY   tuning
to clouds and
        headlights sweeping
constant

in the net.   The birds flutter
        and fling

shattering into,
        and now
  we have no
        unified account of

They say of it: the light was purple and shining
or there was no light or
it became all day.

Some of them caught
in humming,

things torn   for air
    or limbs
        to get through

        atomic despair

Projected, as when figures are called
to surface density in
    plastic undulation. Out of
          color or no other
elemental. Toward the essence of noon

but tendered a ululation of gold, feather
painting, cracked eyes.

So we say to the stillness   now flower,
we are alone under
    a blue
  calling and

wick of air beating air
over the fractional covering

though fraught
     with edge

the music is south now
clouds down and
    the aching jewel
riddles on.

We are disintegrated
to its keeping

of each time and
      the old ideas of form following
a different edge, sharp
     in the waning

though we fold
us under.   Vibrant streamers.

The shadows have gone

Patterns on the siding,
          amber waves of
decibels to perform the particles

a waking   as if we slept,
here, street going on before

as the street
          goes on
                    in moments
of reverberation

THE WHAT GONE SYMPTOMATIC
in the orchid-body—seed-vessels produced
in the beholding of wrapped-in resolution

cruelly deferred by sepals clenched
over the fringing lip. By the way the nude has of talking
her way out of her body, out of the vacant lot caught in dialogue—

helixed, irreproachable, for with respect to the average body
or seeds per capsule, hardly anything need be said—
we've been pressed into capital arms. This

is the way to light us unto, to form us into
the polis of brick and holding, the way marked by the white
of a path through the green, or the shadow

of light scaling her body as she reclines in classical pose. Held
here as the horse in the burning shed, these are remembered
antidotes for the body, for the politic hand holding us here

in a resolution—stopped in a turn
and a counting of sands, dunes eternally shifting, the thought implied
in secreting images, marble statues half buried in siftings

of the elemental in-curling, as the petal-wing curves over egg cells,
as her arm curves, never to be gotten of the origin again, gold
leafing off and into air. We have been left, bare stone, in this dispersal

of the regime, accent placed and displaced upon
what we were pictured holding: the basket of apples changed to a child
over-pink and moving into a solid state of metal, the gun

firing out orange blossoms into the flock held captive, sparks or bullets
becoming the progeny of birds burst into the shadow
of coined knowledge. Of the electric blooming-off of the creator

of the nude body reclining, he lights her hip,
thigh, holding the shadow
in the pocket of his hand to be cupped—as in a window,

as in a seeing into other windows, and the words
crisp to be held and labored over, as the image
of her dressing, and the buttons—one and one—

slipping into their woven nooses,
in orchid-light, or in what is the means of caring,
of carrying on into dusk or the tarmac we have paved over sands—

WORKING AT THE LIP OF EXERCISE with the addition
of this knowledge to the picture we find
we have emptied it

and in our new anthropology of transcendence
the words on the vine shift
under their own weight, character of walking
through water, we become

susceptible to the iron rod, destroying
the interior holdings of the rose, the petal's curve
into stem and vase. Numbers
flood the screen eradicating vision
with a code for policy

and masking determined to make sense
of the smoke billowing against sky. Petals scatter
as our words continue into the space
behind the high wall in the dream

where perhaps we live twinned, hovering
over our own bodies as we wake and move
from room to room following the path
of the sun. Charted outward, are we beholden

to love the world our words made? The images
on the flat surface fold into our story
of the unique idea constituting this country bathed
in heralded light and betrayed by its people's decision.

Our past is organized into possessions
of the verb or the mind furling out
over the mouth of the metro and the glittering stream
of people exiting their city. Their pact

is a critique of what has brought us
to this mode of action, we expect to come
into a new condition when we alter
our position on event, the clouds having been seeded,
our genetic constitution mapped and awaiting alteration

Sound and Image Accordance Two

IN THE HOUSE of some subject, some manner
of breeching, keeping the blue
in my mind while an addition of yellow
adds to green, I am

implied in this message to arms and can feel
someone's impending death
though I cannot claim
their degree of heat
or the red light of distance

lingering at the window
in the nervous hour
of abandoned chair
and gutted building. Am I in the step
of sun mentoring the day in,
a folding. Or in a flooding

off shore, this city of grid and artery mapped
and charted, no longer the same
after blast and drill—
for the medium of the mountain
has disintegrated, and the blue sky cover, sooted

in this sequence of buildings, air
and repetition disappearing, and then, I am I,
magnetite in the mind,
homing. Or have I left

myself abroad, and vast, in
many acres, stepping as some of us
through the air, and through
the relations of one
to one, the pour of machines,
my time marked in taking

AERIAL FORMS grown heavy with
the coast breaking
from itself across cliffs. Instruction
embedded in our spheres, mapped and bolted
to truth in casing though there is still

an opening in day, material of semi-
transparence, the shiver of craft, hand, wing
unfolding to the feast
in this world, of this hour,

the motion sound of shell, sand
grinding us down, the want
centered in a mode of tarrying:

layers peel to discover movement,
a singular tune of questioning

the motion-mind blurs of sun
in the eye, becoming question and
pieces penned against inner foils of
tin cans crushing, against general thought

which is not cognition: flag waving, volume
overcoming perch, mind. In through

the center we valley at the wake's
edge, search for sails, etcetera, the syntax
providing little lead, edge of us, circumference

of sun needed for eyelet, light
penetrating under
branches. To this

illumination (I am I) over grain
and the remembered park, the green

back of the beetle, holding

and this is held, a beginning
into counting, the window
emitting of scales of light, pinked, purled

into what is promised to our spheres, worlds
mapped out under the new flowering of metal—
this is a theme of

branches and a drying bite to the air. In here

there is a blending of singularity, the light
I see by changing from blue-tint to blue

mocking the vapor, air, petal unfurling
then falling, ground down, (I am I)
and the tree withstands the mind dissevering, movement

necessitated by tide, mood, strength
of sun : repetition, bothered by, what has fled

this sense of self, essence
and barrier of pushing past. Machine eye. Pond
in the corner of the field,

I am blue into the instrumental meadow:
houses beyond: casual

conversation in iteration of the Cartesian, world
flux of stepping out of the body,

the baby held: idea intended to stand

dismantled unto a new weathering

as in sea walls, as in precisions: another: one-
another tarrying against, where the boat falters,

when the worlds stream through noise
of silence. Outside and

the escape is green

A SCUDDED FACET OF WHAT WAS tried and the wind

so loud through acres, billowing as we watched

the tossed heads of flowers, and over edges, the harmonics

breaking as in the stream of lightning caught

up around power lines and the birds, here,

unnatural, hovering, over this blood-letting, the unknown

back on the line with a message: someone is wading

into a desert of abandoned light

FOLDED THROUGH THIS aisle secretly,
wishing our bones to remain hardened
in wind, for our bodies are constituted bodies
and we seep—though in this other version
the feel of linden, grove, solidarity
of standing in the sun—light
lidded. To have walked

in the shuddering breeze
for a reason and the sad waves of it,
air twisting banners.
Impression. Of the sweet march,
cake, hands held to the heavens
that will not be promised into. This

has come to a branching, given
in writing to health,
to the life of the tree in lifting. In listing
here despite the copper tower

disrupting the hedge of mountains, blue-bannered sky.
It was and it is so, the story not to be told
because it has come out folded, melody lost, left
to face another direction, and we are only two

passing, a tolling of bells
as if in a medieval city,
crier, town spire. This
burgeoned from the personal day,

signing the contract, contracting
so tightly that I out at the edges—
the breath—the song let loose—

And so unto the electrical bells, sing,
washing over bones to heaven,
heart to earth. Not any other way
to do it, though the hand aches
from holding and
elemental of the heart: hooded.

To the chapel, then, of sand,
over the rose-lit fire of buildings
lift us our eyes

lidded and seeping. To be kindly
and wonder at—how here in this house
of marching and not waiting,
to have been won over by wind,

silk lifted over decision.
Elemental of the heart, mind, hand,
or the waving of us
into a series of gold-tones
layered over gray. A city's song

of the wedding of hand to, and held to—
it is so, as the end of the banner,
untied at the corner and whipping

THE MOUTH having
fallen apart. Ragged
in sections, we have become
what we were meant
to become, internally. Not
that this is now loved
and honored less, but loved

and looked at, it burns.
All we cannot answer
is something about
the eternal, the many
thwarted of sun-beams.
Claiming this, my phrase
is so slow
in the making, a lazy eye. Here

in the middle
of the geometric flower
you scrape at it as
you scrape at us
down streets and.
And feeling

it, isn't it too bad,
though can you see
over the line of buildings
touching buildings, a space
the sun feeds into living

volume, loud and running
to the seam of it.
We are gone now
or going into the stream
of this and this
is not that. The way
of telling it red
and in quarters not satisfied

with the mixing
of elementals. I could
give you the floor-plan
but it wouldn't explain
the way these walls
were erected, and now
by some theory, falling
as in her scarf
flapping through air
to the rusted

sky-line, a refusal
to arrest into meaning
for you, not that I care not
for the blue in it
or the order. Your order

my planning arms
and the words float,
tilt through air. Something
about space and
safety, girders
while they still hug, not yet
disassembled to wait
in a warehouse. This is

the moment
of category, the image
red and palpitating
on wind and I
can say *wind* and
and. That
is about all though
supplied with mirrors
I breathe, and I assure you
something happens

MAKES ME FEEL I'm up in the eastern mountains
released over knots of valley-light, disintegrated
into the many made of smoke plumes, flares billowing

as if we were an array of dawns or another kind
of knowing, interiors blowing toward muscle
and thigh. This is not an apotheosis of the clock,

not a variegated sky or any other set of batteries
writing the line of time from what pressures
the inside, interiors blown toward pen

and word and eye editing in a fluorescence
no longer part of the mountain made of muscles.
Or made of this climb. Our flight has become

beholden and written for the trill and rasp
belonging to grand monuments bowed sideways
toward fading elements of rock and skin

though in a different direction we know this bird
cannot be described in words, etc. We can only see
its shadowy projection on the building, twittering

then stalled in a muscular turn to the tune
of eternal snapping, the spatial elements flown
from the geometrical plain of the mind.

THE COOL OF EVENT and the hovering of us
into what has been described as nothing or being spaced between.
The finished and the legacy of what has been done,
illusion and a darkening around edges, some other counted
into our own periphery becoming a quantity and moving
towards flowers fading into the face of the photograph

caught in a sentence. This is an old house, angled,
akin to wanting letters gilded or hand-crafted
as in his beautiful books or the Bible project,
patented moth wings. This is heat to call
us forth and I hover over my own body slowly walking
up the hill. That he could name the ridges or recite the names
of the ridges, a wondering near to or far to. And hand held to.
And the bells on the corners of the flags. This is extension

or intention born of emptying out
yet still the daughter of agency, coined as a gift, whorled up
in the middle. Lands of mind, digested, asked
to the corners of the valley and I have come
to the top of myself, cranium, dome, ridging

beholden to movement, stretching thought along rooftops, this
is the tree line from my window, my view to become accustomed to
but not to hold, as in the cracked leather glove
held to the nose, its character inhaled, blood beating at the neck,
bird sound beating. Rather, air and into and thusly and we go
and tomorrow and horizon and molecule and, as in a seed pod, up

to take time on this branch of being, not cordoned off
to utter meaning or sound, but dry
as the empty lake, and deep, and waiting late summer rain
to darken the bark of aspens, approximating their scars run through
with silver. Over ends and my beginnings I fold

into the blue texture of the porch at night. A flood of moth
and wing retained, this is the moment burning dark lists
which are separated into great and small and holding or letting go
of this place, an opening of hands. Here there is agency and edges bevel.
Uttered of it. Of us, the slice of day left to shadow down

KARLA KELSEY was born and raised in Southern California. With degrees from UCLA, the University of Iowa Writer's Workshop, and the University of Denver, she teaches at Susquehanna University in Pennsylvania. She lives with her husband Peter on the banks of the river.

Ahsahta Press

SAWTOOTH POETRY PRIZE SERIES

2002: AARON MCCOLLOUGH, *Welkin* (Brenda Hillman, judge)

2003: GRAHAM FOUST, *Leave the Room to Itself* (Joe Wenderoth, judge)

2004: NOAH ELI GORDON, *The Area of Sound Called the Subtone* (Claudia Rankine, judge)

2005: KARLA KELSEY, *Knowledge, Forms, the Aviary* (Carolyn Forché, judge)

NEW SERIES

ED ALLEN, *67 Mixed Messages*

DAN BEACHY-QUICK, *Spell*

BRIGITTE BYRD, *Fence Above the Sea*

LISA FISHMAN, *Dear, Read*

PEGGY HAMILTON, *Forbidden City*

CHARLES O. HARTMAN, *Island*

SANDRA MILLER, *Oriflamme*

ETHAN PAQUIN, *The Violence*

LANCE PHILLIPS, *Corpus Socius*

LANCE PHILLIPS, *Cur aliquid vidi*

HEATHER SELLERS, *Drinking Girls and Their Dresses*

LIZ WALDNER, *Saving the Appearances*

MODERN AND CONTEMPORARY POETRY OF THE AMERICAN WEST

SANDRA ALCOSSER, *A Fish to Feed All Hunger*

DAVID AXELROD, *Jerusalem of Grass*

DAVID BAKER, *Laws of the Land*

DICK BARNES, *Few and Far Between*

CONGER BEASELEY, JR., *Over DeSoto's Bones*

This book is set in Apollo type
with Bauer Bodoni titles
by Ahsahta Press at Boise State University
and manufactured on acid-free paper
by Boise State University Printing and Graphics, Boise, Idaho.
Cover design by Quemadura.

AHSAHTA PRESS
2006

JANET HOLMES, DIRECTOR
AMY GARRETT-BROWN
ABSOLOM J. HAGG
MICHAELA HERLIHY
ADRIAN T. KIEN
TIMOTHY D. ORME
AMY WEGNER, INTERN
ABIGAIL L. WOLFORD